Flying Jewels

A Hummingbird Story

Marta Magellan

by **Marta Magellan**

illustrated by **Mauro Magellan**

Eifrig Publishing LLC

Lemont   Berlin

Cover and book design by Tamian Wood www.BeyondDesignBooks.com

Published by Eifrig Publishing,
PO Box 66, Lemont, PA 16851, USA
Knobelsdorffstr. 44, 14059 Berlin, Germany.
For information regarding permission, write to:
Rights and Permissions Department,
Eifrig Publishing,
PO Box 66, Lemont, PA 16851, USA.
permissions@eifrigpublishing.com, +1-814-954-9445
Library of Congress Cataloging-in-Publication Data
Magellan, Marta
Flying Jewels, A Hummingbird Story/
by Marta Magellan
p. cm.
Paperback: ISBN 978-1-63233-313-1
Hardcover: ISBN 978-1-63233-314-8
eBook: ISBN 978-1-63233-315-5
[1. Nature - Juvenile Nonfiction. 2. Animals - Birds,
Mammals, Pollinators - Juvenile Nonfiction
I. Magellan, Mauro, ill. II. Title
25 24 23 22 2021
5 4 3 2 1

Printed on recycled PCW acid-free paper.

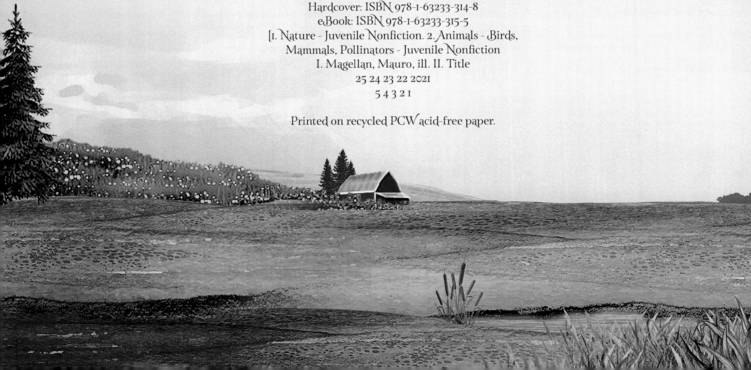

Dedication

As always, in honor of Sammy Joseph Schnall

Science Editors

Deanne Endrizzi, wildlife biologist of the U.S. Fish and Wildlife Services and member of the Minnesota Ornithologists Union

Brian Rapoza, author of the bird-finding guide Birding in Florida, a Tropical Audubon Society Field Trip Coordinator, and a former environmental science teacher at MAST Academy.

A tiny bird flits through a meadow of wildflowers.

Iridescent feathers flash in the sun.

His throat glitters as brilliant as a ruby.

He flies forward, backward, upside down.

A sip here, a sip there, a hundred sips.

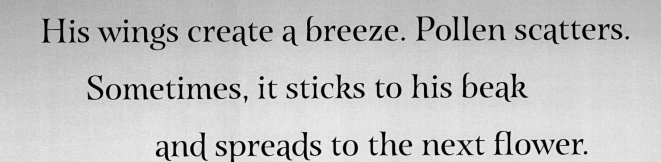

His wings create a breeze. Pollen scatters.
Sometimes, it sticks to his beak
and spreads to the next flower.

With his help, gardens and meadows bloom.

But now, there is a nip in the air.

Ruby-throated Hummingbird must leave.

Seeing the tiny birds for the first time explorers from Spain called them **flying jewels.**

8

English speakers heard their wings beating.
A continuous WHIRR,
a long HUMMMMM
and called them

hummingbirds.

9

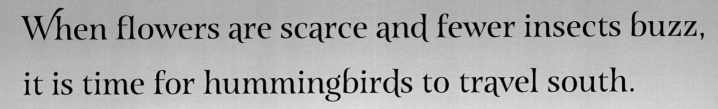

When flowers are scarce and fewer insects buzz,

it is time for hummingbirds to travel south.

Alone.   Always alone.

It is safer that way.

A flock would be too easy to spot.

For such a tiny bird,

danger is always

looming.

II

Look out, Ruby!   ZOOM!

The American Kestral wants a snack

and flies too close!

Ruby-throated whizzes away

12

as fast as a car on a
neighborhood street,
thirty miles an hour!
His wings beat fifty,
sixty times a second.

His speedy flight
made him hungry.
A feeder in someone's yard!
He doesn't notice
the danger
below.
Long, slender bill,
and grooved tongue
reach for sweet nectar.

POUNCE!

15

WHEW!

The feeder was too high for the cat.

Another narrow escape.

After so much flying, so many miles,

he hears the buzz of insects.

Hungry for more than nectar, he needs protein.

A little bee!

SNAP!

But he is not in his territory.

17

SWOOP!

A Rufous Hummingbird appears,
    glowing like a new copper penny.
He spreads his wings
      and points his bill like a dagger.
With angry chirps, Rufous dives at the intruder.

Hummingbirds do not share.

Ruby-throated continues his journey.

He is searching for the Gulf of Mexico,

to a land filled with bugs and blooms.

Where are the vast blue waters of the gulf?

He flies over Florida,

where the sun works long hours.

But not always.

A storm looms in the distance.

21

The clouds burst into a storm.

Wind and water assault the little bird.

Weighing only slightly more

than a penny, he struggles.

His wings too wet, too heavy, slow him down.

The wind has blown him off course.

He is weary.

And lost.

23

24

Finally, the rain stops.

Now it is dark.

The tiny bird has flown a long way

and settles on a branch.

His feathers fluff. His eyes close.

His heart no longer beats 1,200 times a minute.

Fewer and fewer beats,

down to fifty times a minute.

He falls into a deep sleep.

He wakes, hungry.

　　Here and there,

other hummingbirds feed.

　　Attracted by the warm Florida sun,

　　　　by the blooms and the insects,

　　　　　he and the other

　　　　lost hummingbirds

　　stay for the season.

When the weather in the north warms up,

when the rains become

too constant in Florida,

when it is time to nest,

28

all the hummingbirds will fly north again.

And Ruby-throated
                Hummingbird will

find a mate.

His mate will lay pea-sized eggs in a tiny nest

no bigger than half a walnut shell.

By herself, she will sit on the nest

until the new birds hatch.

Iridescent feathers will appear

on the fledgling hummingbirds.

And finally, they too, will grow into

flying jewels.

The Ruby-throated Hummingbird

- The Ruby-throated Hummingbird is the only species that nests in the eastern half of North America.
- The male's brilliant red throat feathers are called its gorget (pronounced gor-jit). Its throat only glitters when the sun hits it just right.
- If the bird is in the shade, or turned away from the sun, its throat appears dark, sometimes even black.
- The female's throat does not gleam ruby red like the male's.
- Most Ruby-throated Hummingbirds struggle on a long 1,500-mile (2,414 km) journey to Mexico and South America. Many brave the nonstop 500-mile (804 km) flight across the Gulf of Mexico to get there.

Ruby-throated Hummingbird by Lindy Lambert

© Lyndy Lambert

Rufous Hummingbird

Rufous Hummingbird
by Frank Cone (Wikimedia)

The Rufous breeds farther north than any other hummingbird in the world. Typically a western bird, it nests as far north as Alaska, but some are now found in eastern North America. It is a long-distance traveler, migrating nearly 4,000 miles (around 6,400 km) from breeding grounds in Alaska to sites in Mexico. During their first winter, inexperienced birds have gotten lost and found their way into nature preserves and gardens in Florida to which they return every winter.

More Hummingbird Facts

⟜ Hummingbirds are only found in the Americas.

⟜ They are the smallest of all birds with over 300 different species.

⟜ They have very short legs, and can neither walk nor hop.

⟜ They hover like helicopters, fly backwards, and even flip upside down.

⟜ Only the females sit on the nest.

⟜ To rest from their long journeys south, they go into a deep sleep called torpor.

⟜ The Bee Hummingbird is the smallest of all birds, just 2 ½ inches (6 cm) long.

Violet Sabrewing
James Gersing

Bee Hummingbird
Charles J. Sharp

Green Thorntail
James Gersing

Other Books from Eifrig Publishing
by Marta Magellan and Mauro Magellan

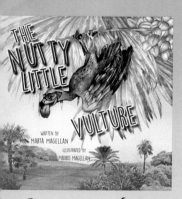

The Nutty Little Vulture

Dragonflies: Water Angels
and Brilliant Bioindicators

Anole Invasion

Felicia and the Rat

Louie and That Dog

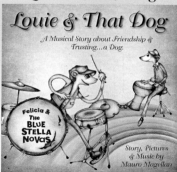

Amazing,
Misunderstood Bats

Acknowledgements

A very special thank-you for the generous members of the St. Augustine Garden Club for providing free books and plants for children during their summer workshops, as well as to the non-profit Random Acts of Reading, supporting creativity, writing, and free books such as these for schools.

Most special thanks to Cathy Snyder whose encouragement and support for pollinators and gardens inspired this and other books in this series and to Anne Crawford for hosting Nature Detectives at the St. John's County Public Library System.

Thank you also to all who helped me review the writing: Silvia Lopez and the members of the SCBWI Coral Gables critique group and for the critiques of my 12 X 12 Online Nonfiction group, especially for the help from Christine Iverson and Kimberly Marcus.